AF317056

Destiny of God's Grace

Ozella Gore

Grace and Merciful Father,
Oh, how I rejoice in Your love.
You are wonders in my life.
My mind is made up!

Hallelujah, glory to God!!!
I thank You for the Blood of Jesus.
I welcome the leading of
the Holy Spirit.

Contents

Open The Eyes of My Heart Lord!

Meaning to open, improve or make possible, access to passage through, to uncover.

Opening of the eyes:

Does your heart reflect your mind? Continual transformation day to day, enlighten to the Word is our beacon of hope and faith. All scripture is given by inspiration of God, and is profitable for doctrine, for reproof, for correction, for instruction in righteous. Create within me a clean heart and renew the right spirit within me.

How can you be angry and sin not? We remember Peter being angry when they came to take Jesus. We remember Jesus in the temple with the money changers.

Is straight-forward truth or gentleness of words seasoned with grace easy? A mentor told me to not give criticism without offering a positive way out.

Prayer: *Lord Jesus, bless me to discern with Your eyes of love. Bless me to be slow to speak and quick to learn to understand. Bless me to study and to be quiet. A quiet and confident spirit God loves. But let it be the hidden man of the heart, in that which is not corruptible, even the ornament of a meek and quiet spirit, which is in the sight of God of great price. (1 Peter 3:4)*

I will praise you with an upright heart as I learn your righteous laws. (Psalm 119:7)

Start day with thanksgiving of grace, mercy, and a song in the morning unto the Lord that it be well pleasing in spirit and truth. (Psalm 92:1-3)

What a beautiful thing, GOD, to give thanks, to sing an anthem to you, the High God! To announce our love each daybreak, sing your faithful presence all through the night. What shall I render to the Lord for all of HIS benefits toward me. (Psalm 116:1)

DESTINY OF GOD'S GRACE

Great are You Lord!!! For as the heaven, are higher than the earth so are my ways higher than your ways, and my thoughts than your thought. (Isaiah 55:9)

Prayer: LORD GOD, please align my ways, heart and thoughts in Your Word that they will be well pleasing to your laws. Anoint my eyes that I may see as you see. Counsel my mind as I listen to Your voice.

And Jesus in pity touched their eyes and immediately they recovered sight and followed him. (Matthew 20:34)

The eyes of the Lord are toward the righteous and his ears to their cry. (Psalm 34:15)

Prayer: LORD, OUR GOD have mercy upon us. May I understand my heart while I empty in your presence. Rejoice in the joy of Jesus through salvation. Salvation is repentance of sin to receive God's forgiveness, compassion, lovingkindness, for HE is faithful and is now able to perform it. The godly profess their confidence in God and pray to be delivered.

Oh Lord my words are limited to express.
I mediate on your Word for correction, deliverance,
victories in your unconditional love daily.

GOD, my Shepherd! I don't need a thing. You have
bedded me down in lush meadows, You find me
quiet pools to drink from. (Psalm 23)

True to Your Word, You let me catch my breath, and
send me in the right direction. Even when the way
goes through Death Valley, I'm not afraid when you
walk at my side. Your trusty shepherd's crook
makes me feel secure.

You serve me a six-course dinner right in front of my
enemies. You revive my drooping head; my cup
brims with blessing, Your beauty and love chase
after me every day of my life. I'm back home in the
house of GOD for the rest of my life!

Psalm 30: You did it! You changed wild lament into
whirling dance; You ripped off my black mourning
band and decked me with wildflowers. I'm about to
burst with song, I can't keep quiet about you. GOD,
my God, I can't thank You enough.

Psalm 31: Be my safe leader, be my true mountain guide. Free from hidden traps; I want to hide in you. I've put my life in your hands. You won't drop me, you'll let me down.

Psalm 31: Be brave. Be strong. Don't give up. Expect GOD to get here soon.

Psalm 29: GOD makes his people strong. GOD gives His peace.

Finally, brethren be strong in the Lord and power of His might.

Psalm 34: GOD keeps an eye on his friends, His ears pick up every moan and groan.

Inspirationals

A Walk of Faith
Life of An Intercessor

An intercessor is one who believes in God's Word,
and labors in the Spirit by prayer.
Feels the burdens of God's desires
for His people.

Sees the need for much unity in the church,
Discerns the evil from the good.
Travails and weeps much for lost souls
and cries out to God for grace
when one is in error.

Lives a pure life before Him.
Quiet and confident in the faith.
Suffers and hurts with the concerns of others.

Is humble, not seeking anything for themselves.
Esteems themselves lower than their
brother to minister to their needs.
Has compassion for others,
Shares unselfishly,

Has words of encouragement
that minister to the heart of man,
and has a very close walk with God.
Listens and rewards openly with the
many fruits of answered prayer.

For this life is hid with Christ, as it so pleases Him.
A life honored by God is one that does not work for
vainglory, but one who has lost his life in Him,
and has been completely crucified in Him.

The honor of an intercessor comes from God,
for it is a reflection of His Son.

A Leader

If you stand alone for a cause
long enough to show your inner strength,
then others will say you were not
born a leader but made a leader.

Being a caring leader will put
brakes on one's own growth.
The pace is slow only because
the leader Has also learned
to be a follower.

Loneliness is a hard test for
strong leadership, but it makes
a confident foundation.

Abide

Endure as a good soldier.
Look up for your redemption is at hand.
When you see the leaves
Off the fig tree a new season is nigh.

Awareness

Feelings are emotions of one's
inner most eyesight of thoughts
to create a state of mind.

Opinions build beliefs,
store up actions as expressions,
confirm feelings loudly or quietly
to display ways of thinking.

Prayer:
LORD, search the intents of my
heart where feelings generate.
Create a clean heart and
renew the right spirit in me.
Amen.

Beloved

Lord, You are awesome!
Unconditional love secretes from
my heart as You create within me a garden of love,
bringing radiance of new beginnings
into a life dedicated to a walk of consecrated
servanthood to fulfill Your will.

Your cleansing blood gently and skillfully
removes memories as you execute
profound heart surgery, cleaning webs
in the gates of my heart.

Deeply, love explores and reflects
You in all Your glory and power.
You inspire me with confidence to
share my complete inner self
with comfort and ease in such
a nurturing way.

DESTINY OF GOD'S GRACE

You supply daily blessings of unspeakable joy,
warmth, and peace that bring out the best
of You in me and me in You as a testimony
of Your grace and mercy.

Surely, Lord, You have done marvelous
things in my life. I reverence Your majesty,
authority, and dominion forever more.
My Beloved!

Ozella Gore

Blessings

GOD, my joy I find within
fountains of youth surely
divine blessings from above.

HE walks with me.
HE talks with me.

Comforter - Almighty King.
Unspeakable joy is revealed
again and again.

I hear His voice from heaven…
Truly my Savior
Blesses me.

Can I Cry? Must I Cry?

A blend of inspiring melodies of instrumental jazz.
The sax, flute, piano whispers soothing, calm
harmony to console a heart once filled with pain.

As laughter swells up from the crest of my heart
a season of intense, bitter, cold, brisk, chilly days
turn into joyous, blissful, radiant sunsets.

Blazing rays of thankful blessings comb the light
blue, orange, yet distant skies, widening the purpose
of my existence, yet soothing the mind with
its bright new dawn.

Gentle, soft velvet clouds embrace the winds
of changes embarking upon my destiny and purpose.
Quietly, a clear stream of salty water glides down
my dark brown cheeks, refreshing me with a
newness of mother earth as it clings for
purity and insight for tomorrow.

Mother earth invites me into a deeper journey.
"Touch me, you've persevered through the darkness.

Daylight will be a breeze".

Ozella Gore

Compassion

A marvelous passion of inner peace, love,
sovereign power, grace, and mercy grant warm,
tender hands to witness forgiveness, kindness,
and tender love from My Lord and Savior
within and My God above.

A once broken, crushed heart,
an intensely bruised spirit with little
fragments of hope, and a tiny measure of faith
trusted in the redemption of unconditional love
flowing oil from the olive branch to heal
and erase self-proclaimed memories of old.

Unspeakable joy takes its place with sacrifices of
praise, worship, and dancing in holy reverence
and fellowship with the Almighty.

Faith pursued freedom within myself,
and I AM found anew, whole, loose, happy,
gleaming, and blessed of light and fire.
It's truly a confirmation that the anointing
of Christ makes the difference.
Jehovah prevails again!

Courage

Courage comes from taking a step
Toward the unknown,
Realizing when a step is attempted
An effort has been made,
And with more courage
One can try again.

Dedication

LORD, I challenge triumph.
Leader, follower, team arise.
Character, efforts, integrity
Come freedom.
I aspire.

Broaden shoulders, brother,
sister accomplish goals.
The cheers and oops ponder not.
It's not the crowd. I must rise.

Excellence, perseverance,
and loyalty wait. Season's over.
I recognize the preeminent seasons.
I understand sacrifices, purpose
blossoms, encourages, enriches
aspirations.

Me.

Despair

Hopelessness streams down into this weary heart
to find a soul full of death and dismay awaiting
strength to leap forth beams of brilliant light
to guide this defeated soul into
its place of peace, happiness,
and purpose.

Cycles of conquests have been so rare,
one questions oneself. Must I go on?
I can't remember the last battle I've overcome.
Unkind afflictions of life form such a
weight of absolute extinction.

Faith has been shattered of all its beliefs
one can only hope for mercy and grace.
A desire for better days seems like a set up for
defeat.

Must I grasp facing another
fall, disappointment, or broken promise.
One questions all beliefs that have
brought one thus far.

Ozella Gore

Ancient spirits tell me it's the love of freedom
you are in pursuit of. It's this freedom that will
heal all injustices you have endured.

Only divine light can free this weary, darkened soul
that lives with such lifelessness. The soul cries out
I must not die here though I've given up.

I must embrace this inner quest, greater wisdom
that will surpass all that I've ever known.
Freedom rings at loud the end of a journey
if I faint not.

Growth pains are crying out.
I, too, must be born.

Destiny

I feel breezes of changes embarking destiny winds of
wisdom empowers transitions on a dusty trail.
One must pursue resilience as courage
swells up within a soul to fight for victorious
revelation visions. One must not retreat.

I welcome prayers to discern quests
to conquer hidden snares set for defeat.
One must seek bravery to cast
upon deep, troubled waters.

By means of elderly counsel,
I trust shoulders to shoulders
Our fights for victories.
We are stronger banded together.

Divine

Divine purpose in one's life
Does not appear in the visible
Sense of God directing that
Person or person into His
Purpose because actions
Are from the intent of the heart,
And only God knows one's heart.

Eye

Teach us your body.
How to war without defeat.
Victory is our focus.
Joy is our strength.
Praise is your command.
Obedience is your way.

Trust and obey
In Almighty God
Through Christ Jesus
Our Savior and Lord.

Flow in the Spirit
As you watch and pray.
Mighty God is He.

My El-Shaddi
Watching over me!!!

Fear

Fear is to be in darkness with no visible direction.
In Christ there is no darkness only light.
That light is revealed to us through His Spirit
Truth awakens to guide
Through his eyes there is no darkness,
and no need to fear.

Prayer:
Lord, fill me with Your Spirit,
lead me and guide me into all truth,
let Your Holy Spirit always abide in me.
Direct my path Lord, that I may see Your
light and walk therein.

Fortitude

Patience - utmost virtue.
Strengths of endurance build visions
with overcoming foundations
bearing fruits for daily blessings.

With patience comes perseverance.
Press on with laps of restoring oils of the
anointing of Christ Jesus
of Nazareth.

Patience brings growing pains of maturity
as ambassadors experience gains wisdom
and wisdom gains knowledge
of applying the Word of the Almighty God
to soar like an eagle.

Thought:
I need your presence, LORD JESUS.

Ozella Gore

Freedom In His Wings

Under the shadow of the Almighty
tucked under His wings in total security
He flies me around in His secret place.
There is no one there but He and I.
We fellowship together.

He lets me know that I am anchored
in the foundation of His Word.
He assures me there is no reason
to fear what men can do to me
for I am completely in Him.

Arrows may fly by day.
Darkness and pestilence may come.
1000 may fall on my right, 1000 at my left,
But – because I am solely trusting in Him,
those things can't touch me or even come near me
for I am wholly in Him.

Freedom

Your uttermost sacrifice of death
Covers boundaries with so much love,
Repentances, deliverances, and praises.

Identity changed. I am free from
Issues of the heart. I found You in me,
Me in You My Saviour and Lord
Jesus Christ.

You are awesome in all Your
Glory, majesty, and dominion.
Praises be unto You
Forever and ever.

Salvation is Free.
Amen.

Gentle Breeze

Blazing rays of thankful blessings
Comb the light blue orange,
Yet distant skies.
Widening the purpose
Of your existence
Yet soothing the mind
Sparkling new gleaming dawn

Glorified

Here I am, Lord, in distress, feeling alone
but yet not alone. Cast down,
but not cast out of Your presence.

Betrayed by some of Your people, yet tucked under
Your wings in security with much needed love.

Stripes of persecution beaten throughout
my flesh, yet glorified in Your eyes for
tasting of that bitter cup.

When men say all manner of evil
against you for my name's sake count it all joy.

When men speak all manner of evil against you
rejoice and be exceeding glad.

Gratitude

Words of inspiration, prayers,
smiles, encouragement,
respect for individuality
I hope I have been transparent
in my time of companionship
with you.

I have come to cherish words
to guide my path of destiny.
May you know I pray GOD's
Abundance for you.

Hallelujahs

Through tribulation there lies a door of freedom.
Outstretch loving, compassionate arms welcome
Jesus' presence, power, strength, purpose,
and refuge.

He calls you by name, _____ and says keep coming.
A new window is opening. It's a heavenly peace.
Take heart and be of good courage.

WE PREVAIL IN HIS STRENGTH...
WE die of ourselves daily to greet the MASTER.
The Highest praise is hallelujah.

Ozella Gore

Happy Anniversary

You come in my life to begin something
wonderful and lovely with exciting memories
as we embrace our hugs, hearts, dreams,
ambitions as fruitful future.

You create within me
feelings I never knew existed
into radiant new beginnings
with comfort, excitement,
and nurturing paths.

Dreams share successes.
Peace calms decisions.
Promises to fulfill.
Insights to make celebrations.
As prosperity flourishes friendships
of loyalty and harmony our hearts reveal
a rich legacy in view.

My love always.

Happy Birthday

As the day approaches warm welcoming smiles
noble character defines the roads leading on a
journey portraits of inner strength
to symbolize beauty.

Happy times friends, hard work, and struggles
frame demeanor, passions, understandings,
laughters and just being nice to family and
fellowman have become your nature.

Years ancestors show forth heritage, intelligence,
wit, harmony, and determinations to inspire and
give insights along this path my spirited legacy.

Wisdom, happiness and peace find places of
harmony and guidance today and tomorrow.

May you enjoy this day from
hearts close to your heart.

Happy Easter

Your uttermost sacrifice of death
covers boundaries with so much love
repentance, deliverance, and praise

My identity has changed
I'm free of the past, failures,
disappointments, and issues of the heart
I'm found anew in me and you in me,
my Saviour and Lord Christ Jesus.

You are awesome in all Your
glory, authority, and majesty.
Praise be unto You
forever and ever.
Salvation is free
Amen.

Happy New Year Embrace

May we embrace peace within while

soaring to gain insight into our purpose.
When God spoke your name from creation
as a "conqueror of your destiny"
LIFE came forth.

Seasons of growth can determine
one's aspirations and fortitude to aim forward.
WE must not sway to the left nor to the right,
but stay strengthened through prayers
and mediations.

In spite of what we see in our everyday life or the
challenges facing our nation this year,
may we remember God is always
one step ahead to prove His power
to the faithful.

Ozella Gore

As we prevail as conquerors
through this year, may our discerning
be sharper than any two-edge sword.
Cowardly or brave motives sometimes can be
deceiving, but if we remember you can't determine
a personality in someone, study an animal
with similar traits and find a treasure of knowledge.

Broaden your shoulders, stand tall, heads up,
feet guided, hearts and minds in tune to God, and we
WIN!!! As we reflect back on this year successes
or perhaps some failures, let's focus on our bright
dawn of this New Year bringing forth many new
beginnings into a prosperous successful future.

Let's aim for unspeakable joy, love,
wisdom, peace, good health and friendships
to enjoy along the way. I pray that we all gain
stronger spiritual awakenings and faith in
knowing the presence of Christ Jesus.
It is because of HIM that I live!!!

Hope

I see you through a pure glass,
reflecting rays of hope.
Through life's many storms
you can bring hope to others.

Hope surfaces from things
thought impossible.
True faith in that hope
brings problems.
Life offers into a walk of peace.

Seek peace above your problems,
and you will find it;
if you only press on with
seasons of enduring power.

Ozella Gore

Image

Resemblance of our Savior
salvation redeems righteousness
and covers behind the cross.

Transformations inside supply
empowerments, strengths,
encouragements, virtues and
compassions giving lights and fire
to endure seasons.

Joy, peace, love fill the
cavities of the humble heart
with promises of continual flows
of our Savior's unconditional love.

The universe reveals God is forever present
and always in tune to His flock.
Jesus tells the Father
I have not lost one soul.

In His Bosom

Life without a problem would not be life,
For Life equals strengths.

Inner life is strength that lies
Within face the storms of life,
For without life and no attempt
To live there is no strength.

A baby cannot eat without a helping hand
Placing bottle in their mouth
For without another life
There is no strength.

Thought:
No one can go through life without
having a problem. Tune into
the source of Jesus Christ
to see the strength.

Ozella Gore

Insecurity

Most easily influenced people feel
Insecure of themselves in areas where
They have little or no knowledge.

They become easily swayed with ideas
That raise the conscious into thoughts
Creating subconscious ideas
That often carry one astray.

Fear causes insecurity of one's ability
To pursue potentials one could
Achieve if not robbed.

Fear says, I cannot overcome this obstacle.
Courage says I can with much effort.
But oh, how often it is so easy to
Never attempt the things one desires
To do in life because of fear.

One may ask, "Where does fear comes from?"
Fear comes from not knowing
The unknown.

Insight

In Christ, the beginning and ending
of all things there is faith.

Faith that in His Word,
when applied to any
situation things turn around.

We all have a horizon
beyond the hills breaking
forth many new beginnings,
wisdom, good success,
health and prosperity.

Ozella Gore

Jewels

Brilliances of gems reflect wisdom,
transformations, abundances of
loving kindness to soften storms
of lives promoting displays of splendor.

Precious stones of vibrant colors reflect
brilliant uniqueness to decorate God's beauty
in the world of his creation.

Rich in the kingdom my Heavenly Father
decorates precious stones with
excellent splendor.

Jewels adorn welcome gates of our
divine home to await our Savior,
saying well done, thou
good and faithful servant.

Joy

Inner peace compass life's many storms.
Love conquers the inevitable
sorrows one can encounter.

Praises fulfill the heart with inspiration of thanks
dancing responses to the knowledge
of knowing the joy of the Lord
is my strength.

Ozella Gore

Knowledge

Knowledge versus error!
Time challenges each one to envision
truth and eradicate insight to define one's destiny.
Lack of knowledge, wisdom, and understanding
defeats one's own purpose of existence.

It demeans one's character, goals and will to live
harmoniously with humankind. Truth equals
fortitude despite the awakenings of self-awareness
as it yet represents noble adulthood.

Search of divine truth equips one walk of life to gain
knowledge, insight, and endurance encouraging rites
of passages to define character, integrity, and
wholeness of oneself.

Absence of knowledge depicts weaknesses,
ignorance, unawareness of identity, truth,
and freedom. Gain truth to envision, eliminate
and empower your calling with
seasons of enduring wisdom.

Learn of Me

My love sees the intent of the heart.
My love looks beyond faults.
My love sees no one as a failure.
My love reaches to the lowest part of
your inner being and says there is hope.

My love says, reach out and touch me,
take my hands in yours.
Together we can go through
anything you have to face.

My love feels your hurts.
My love will embrace you in
the midst of life's many storms.

My love sees your tears
streaming down your face and says,
trust Me, talk to Me, let Me help.

My love says, keep coming to me
for I have much to share with you.
My love says, I have all things in control.

Thought:
To learn of Christ, you have to share
all of you with Him.

Liberation

My curiosity of yesterday's fears transform a
freedom of today's dreams to emancipate
a bold, courageous wholesome heritage.

I will not pace with dismay, nor dread its challenges
but embrace every walk of opportunity as a bridge
perfecting my thoughts, will and purpose linking
failures with successes
To celebrate whom "I AM".

Rebirth grasps my intellect as "I AM"
aims toward infinite wisdom, unspeakable truth
and a freedom of choice unshackling the
chains of the past as I discern, confront and achieve
deep revelations to remedy a dusky trail.

I validate my own existence as liberty beholds my
tenacious character I'm confident in knowing
Who "I AM", what I resemble and who I aspire to
become I don't need someone else to define for me
who and what "I AM".
I Am a Child of God!

Longsuffering

Resilience symbolizes perseverance
towards possibilities wisdom weathers the storms.
One's demeanor cultivates strength and beauty
understands courage, expresses knowledge,
brings forth maturity.

Warm smiles and eyes symbolize a rich life.
Core reflections, rays of sunshine
a friendly solid pillar of love to encourage.
Character stands tall, shoulders square
and erect represents lifelong lessons.

Prayer:
Lord, teach me how to press toward the
mark of the high calling of Christ Jesus.

Ozella Gore

Motivation

LORD, I attempt to conquer challenges, fears, and
disappointments as I learn what a leader, follower
and a team can accomplish together.

I understand it's all about effort, character,
and integrity. I aspire to stand to build up
my brother and my sister as we labor
to win and accomplish our goals.

The cheers and oops I must not concentrate on.
It is not the crowd I desire to please; it is myself.
I must arise for excellence, dedication
and loyalty for the occasions.

When this season is over I know I gave my best.
I understand myself better too, and what
sacrifices are all about.

I've learned valuable lessons that have inspired me
as a student of life aspirations to continue growing
and blossoming into my mold of existence.
I'm encouraged to know me.

My Closest Friend

My closest Friend had so much love for me
that He could see no fault.
When I did something without control
I was forgiven without reservation.

When sorrow and disappointment grasp hold of me
I cried to my Friend and He helped me.
When no one seemed to care my Friend
never left me, not even for a moment.

When crying was all I knew to do about
the burdens I carried, my Friend said,
"Give them to Me, for I care so much for you
that I will carry them for you.".

When life's past haunted me, my Friend
said He held it not against me
for it was another life.

When I was rejected, my Friend said,
"Cheer up, I have been there too."
I have overcome.

Ozella Gore

When no one was there to listen,
with understanding, my Friend taught me
to rest in Him, for He truly cares for Me.

When pain gripped by body
My Friend held my hand and let me
know His Grace is yet sufficient.

When courage seemed to be slipping
from me, my Friend said,
"Stand Still, and know that I am
standing with you. His strength braced
my legs with hope.

When my mind seemed so consumed
and there were no words to utter,
my Friend said, wave your hand for
that blesses Me.

When persecution came, He blessed me with family
and friends who held me up in prayer and said,
"Run on, for I AM with You."

It was then, I realized my closest Friend
had united me with true brothers and sisters.

DESTINY OF GOD'S GRACE

When I had to walk alone, He took my hand,
and we began to walk as One.

My closest Friend arose from death to
prepare a place where we could
spend eternal life together.

I await the day of His return to see Him as He is!
Jesus, I Love You, for You are truly
my closest Friend.

Ozella Gore

My Heart

Feelings are one's innermost thoughts
created into emotions.

Emotions create actions
wherein feelings are stored.

Feelings are emotions
one possesses and
relates to others.

Prayer:
Lord, search the intent of my heart
where feelings are generated.
Jesus, create in me a clean heart
and renew the right spirit in me.
Amen.

People

People are trying constantly to be or to do things
to get respect from people, when if they would be
honest people, meaning the person they really are,
then they would get respect from their peers
and others without being deceitful.

Life is made up of two kinds of people.
People who are honest. Meaning ones who get
across the things on their minds and remain honest;
People who are not honest. Meaning ones who act
dishonest to gain standings whether small or large
without being concerned for others.

People should realize that they are living behind a
face that is not theirs when they are not honest.
It means they are keeping themselves from
becoming mature, honest adults that would make
life and others around them more bearable.

Life can be simple, if taking the time.
Life can also be complex,
if in fact people don't express
their true feelings and take the courage
to make some serious changes within themselves.

Perfect

In Christ, the beginning and end of all things
is faith in His Word, when applied to any situation,
will turn things around into His perfect plan.

Christ being perfect in all His ways suffered on the
cross perfectly. He saw you and me in sin,
lost with no hope of redeeming ourselves.

Yet one by one, He took long nails in the
center of His hand, long nails in the
tenderness of His feet, spear torn in His sides,
sharp needles of thorns in His head.

Hair plucked from His face, strips of flesh beaten out
of His back, clothes stripped from His body,
— all in the midst of a crowd, showing forth
perfect love for all mankind.

Perfect Love said, if they look at me and see
that I died this cruel death, that they would live with
me one day, they would know by laying down
my life I love them!

Thought:
Greater love hath no man than this,
That a man lay down his life for his friends.

Praises

Out of abundances of my heart
You bless me by name.
Oh! How I worship you my
King and LORD.

I bathe in Your name.
Refresh my body, soul, mind, and spirit.
Let fountains of You in Your Word
Stir up praises to please You today.

Ozella Gore

Precious

As tears vanish in the night daybreak teaches
loving memories will calm this too.
Our talks, whispers of your sweet loving,
gentle voice warm hearts so dearly.

Precious love, words of wisdom, laughter
welcome open doors of your heart full of gold.
Precious strength during weak moments
teach me endurance is our legacy.
I remain strong in firm foundation.

My dearest precious friends sat at Your loving feet,
with loving outstretched arms uniting moments
of funny gestures into generous wisdom
to share happiness.

You met no stranger without welcome smiles.
My dedication to fulfill visions, inspire generations,
warm hearts, enjoy friends with pleasant
conversations will always symbolize you Precious.

You rest now in the loving arms of Jesus.
I Love You, Precious.

Provision - Joy

Verse 1

GOD is my joy, unspeakable joy.
He walks with me. He talks with me.
The Almighty King, I hear His voice
from heaven above. Truly, Jehovah Jireh
is blessing me!

Verse 2

GOD is my refuge.
My present help
in the time of trouble.
I trust in Jehovah Shammah.

Verse 3

(Sinners)
Do you know Jesus
in the pardoning of your sins?
If so, give Him praise!
For truly, God is worthy to be
praised!

Verse 4
God is Joy Unspeakable JOY!
Inside the fountain of youth
Lies blessings from above.

Blessed is the Lamb of God
Jesus is His name.
Worthy to be praised!

Verse 5
Jesus my king.

Quietness

Lord, daily intimacy asks decrease inside me,
increase your gardens of love.
I desire, I hunger, I listen, I know
new mercies await every dawn.
I choose to witness utter forgiveness.
Victory is mine.

As time goes by I'm blessed.
Lord not as man sees or we see others.
Redemption celebrations within
reveal a close relationship
in your eyes of love.

By name _____, He says
I have so much compassion for you
so much grace for you. So much patience for you.
Mercy speaks I will not fail you.

By name _____, He says, I Love You!

Release Me

Your inner court is the habitation
wherein is Your presence I'm welcomed to
worship You in all of Your glory.

Your presence invites me to bathe in riches,
fills unconditional love, sanctification, and holiness.
You counsel my soul, mind, and spirit.

Light speaks and tabernacles shining
upon paths directing ordered steps.
I've touched the hem of Your garment.
You have made me whole.

I bow at Your presence. I reverence the holiness of
Your majesty. I feel enlightened revelations.
Beacon beams upon a vessel.

Intimate being witnesses love of freedom,
searches of a lifetime. It's a treasure I embrace so
dear life itself all wrapped in You.
I've been released into a sanctuary,
fellowship and communion
true praise and worship.

Respect

Respect is listening to someone's opinion
Before making a judgmental decision.
Respect is being open to criticism
Without always taking an offended attitude.

Respect is reflections of one's ideas
To balance out indifference of
One's opinion over another.

Without respect for other people
Respect has no value to anyone.
Respect is not given.
Respect is earned.

Ozella Gore

Rock of Ages

Salvation lights fire, transform abundances
of loving kindness softening storms of lives
promoting unity in the Body of Jesus Christ.

Warmth of flowing love reaches, embraces,
reveals Heavenly Father like honey.
A sweet aroma in His nostrils,
well pleasing to His sight.

Savior symbolizes rock of origin.
Precious gems, foundations, priceless treasures,
a devoted whole heart, a reflection of his Kingdom.

Abba Father precious gems decorate
the courts of sanctuaries pleasing instruments
beautiful to the world.

Jewels adorn the welcome gates
our heavenly home
forever.

Royal Priesthood

The likeness of His Son
Reflects true ownership of the soul.
Salvation supports the robe of righteousness
covers the ministers of God behind the cross.

Transformation inside supplies
Empowerments, strengths, encouragements,
Virtues and compassions giving light and fire
To endure rites of passages.

Everlasting joy, loving kindness fill the
Cavities of the humble heart with promises
of continual flowings of His spirit.

The universe reveals
God is forever present
And always in tune to
His flock.

My El-Shaddi

Ozella Gore

Rubies

The brilliance of rubies reflect
wisdom, transformation, consecration, light, and fire.
Words with the abundance of loving kindness soften
the storms of lives, promoting unity of true
sisterhood in the Body of Christ.

Warmth of flowing love perspire an embracing of the
Heavenly Father like honey gently running down His
fingers sending a sweet aroma to His nostrils
pleasing in His sight.

The value of rubies are far greater than coral and
jasper and comes from creation, destined to
conquer. Rubies with the Master's anointing comes
from the same rock of origin.

Precious stones of this deep red color are rare and so
special to GOD as they represent a devoted whole
heart as a reflection of his SON from within.
Gold cannot be compared to it's worth.

DESTINY OF GOD'S GRACE

Rich in the Kingdom of My Heavenly Father
these precious stones have been refined
to decorate the courts of the sanctuary
to regard highly as a pleasing instrument
of GOD's beauty to the world.
Rubies adorn the welcome gates
of our heavenly home
a delight to see.

Ozella Gore

Search Me

Lord, I stand before You unclothed,
Hiding nothing.

Search my feelings and thoughts,
Desires and wants.

Guide me to perfection.

Servant's Kneel

It's with humility, meekness, and adoration
I lie at my Master's feet clothed in earthly apparel.
I serve for a heavenly robe dipped
in the Savior's cleansing blood
for the cross I bear.

It's not the brutal stripes I've endured,
the scandals I've lived through,
the disappointments, falls, and
brokenness I've witnessed in my life.
I celebrate Jehovah Shalom is with me.

It's another day that demonstrates
Faithfulness and honor from my LORD!
I persevere in faith, hope, and charity
in a lowly state of mind to love the
body of Christ Jesus.

I pray Jehovah Jireh rewards all my
labor of love efforts to promote the ministry
of the saints toward holiness,
boldness and unity in this life's time.

Ozella Gore

I'm a servant kneeling unashamed LORD,
pleased to serve in the fellowship, reverence,
and anointing of Almighty God.

Yet modest and brave I desire strength
to fulfill my mold of existence
as an example of true courage
of a yielded vessel.

Shepard's Heart

The likeness of Your Son
Reflect true ownership of a soul.
Salvation supports.
Robes of righteous covers
Ministers of God behind the cross.

Transformations equip empowerments,
Strengths, encouragements
Virtues and compassions
Giving lights and fires
Enduring awakenings of passages.

Everlasting joy, loving kindness
Fill cavities of a humble heart
With promises, continual flowings
Jesus anointing oils.

The universe reveals
God's forever presence
Is always tuned
To His sheep.

Ozella Gore

Stand

Reputation in awe of truths, efforts,
and foundations become inner strength,
and endurances.

Upright aloneness proves mountain walks of faith.
Heartfelt love of God conquers doubts and worries.

Observers test character, patience as one learns,
reflects, understands perseverance and
discipline towards what seems impossible.

Leadership is a hard lesson and
reveals one must encourage himself
or herself in the midst of it all.

Alone on the front lines at your weakest moments
With no one encouraging you, that my friend is
ambitions and godly senses of purpose
warrant loneliness yet the hardest task,
stand again.

Success

I'm motivated to aim for excellence.
I'll eradicate, educate, envision and empower
knowledge to understand the path of life's
aspirations, achievements, and adversities
as I develop maturity into noble adulthood.

Rites of passages question me to define character,
integrity, cultural awareness, spiritual awakening,
compassion and self-worth to become a conqueror
of one's struggle for existence.

My parents, mentors, and teachers did not teach me
to detect motives, to define winners or losers,
brave or cowardly attributes as I become a
champion of my destiny to fulfill
the mold of my origin as only I can.

Wisdom enfolds inner strength
as a conquest to brave peace in the midst
of life's rites of passage toward a future of
prosperity, distinguishing and affirming
absolute identity, truth, and freedom
to merit the beginnings of success.

Ozella Gore

Suffering

Knowing who you are in Christ
makes all the difference. It is the key.
What does it mean to suffer in and for Christ?
To stand for the truth, steadfast,
unmovable in the faith?

Persecution comes when you take a stand for what
you believe, and others who have not
come up to par see their shortcomings
and try to discredit you.

If their light is not shining as bright as another,
their objection is to dim that light
by constructive criticisms.

When, if they would acknowledge
where they are in the walk, and try to get to
that place in Christ; unity
would be as it should.

Strength would be in the church.
Deliverance would reach the captives and
freedom through God's Word would
keep souls in the church.

Take not the offensive when you
are a sheep in the midst of wolves,
But count it all joy, and rejoice in
knowing you are suffering for the
gospel of Christ and not yourself.

Ozella Gore

Thankful

A spirit of hope.
Words of joy.

Inspirations to remember,
Wisdom to define,
Success to achieve,

Moments in time
A spirit of excellence
I find in you.

I am thankful to God,
His treasure in you.

The Tongue

Through life's many trials
We are beaten with stripes on the back.
Blood running down (backbiting)
Tender to touch (wounded)
Slapped on the face (betrayed)
Broken spirit (aching heart)
Despised with no one to listen (rejected)
Pushed aside (lonely)
An untamed tongue.
How great a matter a
little fire kindleth!

Prayer:
Lord, tame my tongue with Your Spirit.
Let it bring forth peace to all mankind.

Ozella Gore

Today, Tomorrow, Forever

Out of the abundance of my heart
You bless me by name.
Oh! How I worship You
my King and Lord.

I bathe in Your name,
Refreshing body, soul, and spirit
Renewed fountains of Your spirit
Inspire my desire to please You on today.

Trust

The beginning and end of all things,
faith in God Word turns
lives victoriously indeed.
What greater love is there?

Why do you love me Jesus?
His answer:
I create love. I generate love.
More than that, I am love.
Trust me.

Jesus is perfect in all His ways.
He died on the cross, rose in three days.
They will know with His life.
He said, I love you.
What greater love is there?

He looks at you and I in sin,
lost with no hope and redeems us
by His saving blood.

Ozella Gore

Unification Uh!

A youthful mind sees earth-tone complexions:
pecan tan, ebony, cocoa, mahogany
light, medium and dark as a bonding
balance of harmony and togetherness.

As time passes on the immature mind
has become dazed and bewildered
of these blended colors of humankind.
Dark circled, saddened eyes filled
from hurtful tears see deception
and discord on every hand.

An overwhelmed, bruised heart
becomes crushed with another's deeds of
mischief, envy, jealousy, and strife.
A troubled soul questions if true brotherhood
has anything to do with one's color or race.

DESTINY OF GOD'S GRACE

A rude awakening takes place.
The illusion of unification based upon one's
color or race now passes by.

An experienced, developed, mature mind
bares a unique awareness of truth now;
yet feels a numbness of its revelation.

Life has taught the child within,
one must pursue enlightenment
through all people without
stained-glass color barriers.

Seeking unity among mankind,
yet realizing until one unveils
and unifies a oneness with one's self
does one possess wholeness and unity.

Utmost Virtue

Patience begets:
Perseverance,
Faith,
Restoration,
Experience,
Wisdom,
Knowledge,
Endurance,
Testimony,
More than
a Conqueror

Prayer:
Jehovah may the fruits of the Spirit
always abide in me.

Victory

I feel the breezes of changes embarking upon
destiny. Winds of wisdom must empower to
weather this dusty trail.

One must pursue resilience as courage swells up
fortitude. A soul listens for revelation
with no vision for defeat.
One must not retreat.

I welcome prayer to discern this quest to conquer.
One must seek bravery to cast upon deep troubled
waters. By means of elderly counsel I trust.
Shoulders to shoulders one fights for
victory as WE are stronger banded together.

Jehovah Nissi will prevail, again!

Ozella Gore

Within Me

Life revolves around discovery of one's self.
It stimulates desires of fulfillment.
It releases quality of love within one's self,

The ability of relating love to others.
Dreams of happiness, and eternal peace
lie within dreams, with tears of growth.

I reach within me and see life in its
fullest blossom giving me
an enjoyable view of all it offers.

Where I admire trees, flowers and earth
in all its natural self and also admire within
the discovery of one's self.

Wisdom

Age has no barrier with God
for we all must come as a child.
No other way can one go to heaven
except as a child.

Wisdom does not lie in age as some suppose.
Wisdom lies in God, and if you are
in Him and seek godly wisdom
you can find it.

Know that what you stand for is the truth.
Be a doer of the truth you proclaim.
A living example will prove what talk can't.

Generations

Torch of Generations

You, our African kings and queens render such
strong spirits, beliefs, sacrifices, memories,
foresights, and prayers into the days and nights as
our guide to walk tall, broaden shoulders, listen
carefully, and declare strong faces as our
responsibility. We must live to live again.

It's in yesterday's view I behold the greatness of
today. Symbols of hope, courage, fortitude, wisdom,
insight, and strength witness walks of firm faith,
struggle, pain, and love.

We bow to your uniqueness of survival.
Rest in your stand for justice as we celebrate strong
traits of family ties gifts from them to you, for us
a brighter, beautiful tomorrow for all.

Let's remember the warmth of smiles laughter in
eyes gentleness of touch words of truth, hearts of
compassion, gratitude for knowing our paths have
crossed with lots of loving memories
as "we" represents "you" "I" represents "us".

Ozella Gore

See I know its fingerprints of your DNA
that run through my veins:
Granddaddy, grandmother,
father, mother,
uncle, aunt, brother, sister,
nephew, niece,
it is you again.

I encircle to light this torch of
"Generations".

Grandmother

The beauty of your gracious gentle smile
warms my loving heart into joyous tears
in celebration of your contributions
into my life.

Just to be in your presence symbolizing
my rich legacy with such strength, courage,
and fortitude gives me so much hope
for my destined future.

You embrace life with such wisdom,
And mannerism showing forth your bravery,
Insight and daring traits for perseverance,
success, and patience.

You inspire me with such silent confidence
to believe in myself, even when I'm standing alone.
To know I'm embraced by your deep passion
of endearment encouraging me to
pursue a fruitful future.

You are the apple of my eye,
always directing me toward a better me.
I pray in my lifetime I will show forth
such a sincere affection for life.

Grandmother,
I love you dearly.

Dedicated To My Mother
Essie Mae Thomas Gore

I find inside this lovely home a pretty,
graceful lady with long curly gray and black hair
who warm the hearts of anyone who visits
from near and afar.

She's truly a missionary of yesterday.
She comforts the sick with smiles,
bowls of homemade soup to make their life
more cozy and hers being extra tired.

She listens to your dreams, your hurts,
and your fears, and tells you to be patient
for life has just begun. God is surely
with you and definitely on your side.

She has several children.
Three daughters and one son.
There is nothing she wouldn't do
to make their lives secure and warm
and share her motherly charm.

Ozella Gore

She weighs their disappointments
with tender and affectionate sweet talks
wisdom, laughter, and good-hearted understanding.

She gives and gives and gives, right down to her
last dime and lots of her time.
She works long hours in the garden
sharing with her neighbors.

She will give you her last bite to make sure
you've had a snack even if she lacks.
Most good Samaritans only come out at Christmas,
but in this home I see this all year long.

She's my mother. Sitting over there
with her warm smile and gentle touch.
She's modest and always giving all of
her affection to anyone in need of some tender love.

Mother of my heart. Mother of my soul.
Mother of godly wisdom.
Mother of my dreams.
Mother of all my compliments.
Mother full of grace.
Mother of warmth,
full of compassion.

Daddy
Tribute Alexander Gore, Jr.

How often your peaceful eyes warm my heart.
Your gentle, calm demeanor listens, soothes,
encourages everyday worries, doubts, and ambitions
with love, patience, understanding and endurance
which seems to be your greatest virtues.

I've learned through your lifelong experiences
time heals hearts when shared with affectionate
compassionate truth.

You listen with understanding, share with a loving
spirit of thoughtful words only a dad can give.
Time has come and gone, yet father relationships
flourish with seasons of encouragements.

I've truly been blessed to
know you as Daddy.

Ozella Gore

My Son

My zeal pampers, loves, nurtures, shares,
and consoles my child, my son. Good judgment, faith,
and joy bring me such fruitful happiness, peace,
laughter and a lineage of confidence, thankfulness,
and trust in God.

A man of respect, hope, and success
will become today…

Show the world your rich heritage.
A joyous birth.
My heir!

My Daughter

My love of you within moments
without measure warms my loving heart
to embrace, welcome and thanks to my God.

My precious little girl, my first glimpse of you
I thought cool pink, lavender, green,
vivid blue skies could only birth
a joyful bliss radiance to mirror
my deep love as I celebrate
my daughter's birth.

Only God above, our creator could
Give me a passion like this!

Ozella Gore

Family

I've been blessed with a
great extended heritage
that supports, unites, heals,
shares, teaches and explores.
I, we, and they.

Tributes

Mourning Later

A cold, damp, crisp,
Breezing wind gently wraps me.
It surrounds me with a sense of familiarity.
Tears begin to fill my eyes as loneliness sweeps my
heart. For someone is near me that I've known
before. I question myself, who could this be?

Days have come and gone now, yet this presence
continues to stay. Surrounding me now with
a sense of warmth and tenderness.
The presence now gets closer.
Its filled with love and yet loneliness too.
I could sense the presence saying I've not been gone
long. Do you remember me and miss me too?

I reverence the presence and reminisce
over our past. I found myself in mourning
again for someone so dearly who has come and
gone. It comforts me to feel this closeness
once again from someone I miss too.

DESTINY OF GOD'S GRACE

As the night gently leaves the bright beaming sunrise
breaks the blue rushing skies to guide the presence
into a world quite different from mine.

I will cherish these memories this closeness too,
as time goes on from someone who continues to
cross the paths of my heart.

Ozella Gore

Tribute to My Mother
Essie

A benevolence of grace
nurture, compassion, tenderness
understanding, loving kindness and
uniqueness fill the frame of my Mom whom
I love, admire, and respect as my parent,
counselor, and mentor.

She promotes character throughout
my life's growth stages for endurance.
She's gifted with wisdom in the midst of difficulties
to support, encourage, and direct
my actions toward true maturity.

She renders precious shoulders to lean on while
wiping my tears when in distress.
She coaches me to strive for life's best,
teaching me some sacrifices
have to be made.

DESTINY OF GOD'S GRACE

As I make mistakes, she embraces me
with reassuring warm tenderness,
showing how failures promote
successes to accomplish a
journey of true harmony.

I salute you, Mother
with a portion of my heart,
devoted only to you.

Ozella Gore

You Were There

When I needed a shoulder
with love and understanding
and tears began to flow we embraced
with tenderhearted hugs rather than tissue.
You were there.

A warm shelter with protection
to lay my head with strength, encouragement
and insight is the dear friend I found in you.

We shared our dreams, aspirations, and family,
for it does take a village of love.
When they said I won't make it
you said, "Z shake it off.
Rise up to the occasion.
We got this!"
We did.

DESTINY OF GOD'S GRACE

When mom talked with you it gave me
a sense of peace knowing all would be well.
My sister, you were there.

My dearest true friend, sister, and mom,
Your genuine love showed me how to live.

Welcome Home!
I live to meet you there.

Love Always!
"Allene"

Ozella Gore

Dad's Hand

Humility, meekness, and salvation
faith, hope and charity, I witness in you.
Solemn trust in God. A gentle calm demeanor
soothes everyday worries.

You counsel with words of comfort
encourages strength and courage
as love flourishes blooms.

Years have come and gone now.
Family ties strengthened, some broken,
yet our hearts share and trust in God,
struggle and love.

You teach be slow to speak, with a caring heart
while time teaches love, patience, wisdom,
and longsuffering great virtues
of a man of God.

I am blessed to witness your
praying hands
for me, too.

Beloved Treasure
Tribute Grandma
"Miss Ruby" McAllister

You embraced life with such feisty wisdom.
Gentle, quite mannerism shows bravery
insights and daring traits.

Just to be in your presence
symbolizes rich heritage.
You would say "I popping today"
I would reply you are truly a fighter,
a tiger for sure of ninety-eight years.

You inspired me with such silent confidence
to believe in myself even when I stand alone.
Talking to you and seeing you clasp
hands on your face as you listen to me
showed loving tender affection.

Ozella Gore

Passions and understanding
showed godly love and forgiveness
will be deeply missed.

You became the wind beneath my wings.
You encouraged me to aim high.
Just to be in your presence
symbolized your rich legacy.

To know I embraced deep passions of endearment
to pursue a fruitful future made me
hold my head high and broaden
my shoulders square.

The beauty of your gracious, gentle smiles,
warm loving hearts to joyous tears in
celebration of your contributions in our lives.
I pray in my lifetime I will show forth
sincere, loving affections you taught me.

"Miss Ruby"
I love you dearly.
You are home now.

Tribute to
Cynthia Ann Bryant
My Friend

How often your peaceful eyes warm my heart
your gentle, calm demeanor listens, soothes,
encourages everyday worries, doubts and ambitions
with love, patience, understanding and endurance
which seems to be your greatest virtues.

I've learned through your lifelong experiences time
heals hearts when shared with affectionate
compassionate truth. You listen with understanding.
share with a loving spirit of thoughtful
words only a friend can give.

Time has come and gone, yet a friend relationship
flourished with seasons of encouragements.
I've truly been blessed to know you as
friend.

Ozella Gore

Tribute to Dr. Will My Friend

It is within your quietness and knowing
who you are that I have come to admire the most.
I know you to be candid and calm. One who has
shown me how to better combat obstacles
I will come to face.

Over the years I have seen you devote
so much time sharing, caring and nurturing others.
It is seldom that one can reflect to others
the genuine father like character
that you so often portray.

You freely give encouragement where there is
despair. It shines radiantly in a cloud
where there is much rain.
Your statue of confidence keeps
others calm when the sea
is steady roaring.

DESTINY OF GOD'S GRACE

It is your listening with concern and guidance
for others that keeps your office filled
with students, both young and old.

Your warmth, kindness, and humor
has shown me not to be so hard on myself,
rather to be determined to preserve
in becoming the person who can be
more than she is, if she only
pursues her dreams.

It is knowing the meaning of true friendship you
taught me that has caused me to value
our friendship even more. It is your hugs of
compassion that help me weather the day
when my eyes are filled with tears.

It is empathy in your eyes I see when I need
understanding. It is talks we have when I
share a part of me and you share a part of you.
This is my friend I have come to know
and love.

Good Morning, Friend
Tribute to Howard Poole

Oh! Our angel watches you,
family members, friends, and loved ones on our
journeys with love, wisdom, strength, and guidance.

Face tomorrow with courage like none other. We
possess memories with truthful, grateful celebration.
Your compassion to face life's challenges with full
zest for life.

He outpoured love for family, friends,
and loved ones to embrace a deeper insight
of someone we will remember throughout the ages.

Our philosopher gave understanding,
patience, and fortitude a deeper guidance
toward our fulfillment and discovery of self.

Time begot Howard's legacy with lovely memories
to exhibit "Howard Poole" our Friend full of life.

Lovely Treasures

Happy Mother's Day "Mrs. Carr"

I see within your genuine smile a gentle soul.
You nurture, embrace, listen and pray with such
grace. I witness years of heart felt love
to impart wisdom in many situations.

Our history symbolizes families much love,
compassion, and trustworthiness to guide.
In despair and grief to listen encourages
words of comfort. You calm me to share
unspoken thoughts.

"Wait on God for healing and guidance for better
days," she says. Inspiration finds me in awe
of a lovely adopted mom's love.

God has given me another Mom indeed.
Love You dearly,
Ozella (Zell)

Happy Mother's Day
"Mother Betty"

Love shines in the eyes of Mother.
Your heart listens to every sigh, laughter, cry,
and prayer. Wisdom lives in the mind
of this genuine soul.

Spiritual guidance, peace, compassion,
godly maturity is by nature the strongest gifts.
"Knowing what's best is always God's way"
is our favorite quote.

Young and old souls alike whisper secrets only
Mother would hold in her heart, right to the throne
of grace and mercy.

Mother gives comfort when nothing else could,
would, or try to show warmth and kindness.
Peace, and joy speak loud in mother
to my heart, to your devoted heart.

We share moments of divine love only God would
allow. I've found treasures in you.
Love You Dearly,
Ozella

About the Author

 Ozella Gore is a resident of North Carolina. Throughout years of God's grace, I've witnessed the love of Jesus Christ as my Savior and Keeper. The redemptive love of Jesus has blessed me with His grace, mercy, and kindness. I'm so thankful I'm saved. My prayer is that someone will see how trials and tribulations are doors. Jesus is saying, "I have overcome, and I love you in the midst of it all." From generation to generation, there lies deliverance, and mercy speaks.

www.ingramcontent.com/pod-product-compliance
Lightning Source LLC
Chambersburg PA
CBHW050737150726
48196CB00003B/246